INTROVERTED
Women
LEADERS

5 INNOVATIVE STORIES ON
HOW TO LEAD AS A "QUIET" WOMAN

BY ADRIANA LUNA CARLOS

ALONG WITH
ANGELA BELL, ALEXIS ENTERLINE,
MICHELLE BELL & STACEY DORENFELD

SHE RISES
STUDIOS

Table of Contents

INTRODUCTION

She Rises Studios was created and inspired by the mother-daughter duo Hanna Olivas and Adriana Luna Carlos. In the middle of 2020, when the world was at one of its most vulnerable times, we saw the need to embrace women globally by offering inspirational quotes, blogs, and articles. Then, in March of 2021, we launched our very own Women's Empowerment Podcast: *She Rises Studios Podcast*.

It is now one of the most sought out Women based podcasts both nationally and internationally. You can find us on your favorite podcast platforms, such as Spotify, Google Podcasts, Apple Podcasts, IHeartRadio, and much more! We didn't stop there. Establishing a safe space for women has become an even deeper need. Due to a global pandemic, women lost their businesses, employment, homes, finances, spouses, and more.

We decided to form the She Rises Studios Community Facebook Group. An environment strictly for women about women. Our focus in this group is to educate and celebrate women globally. To meet them exactly where they are on their journey.

It's a group of Ordinary Women Doing EXTRAordinary Things.

As we continued to grow our network, we saw a need to help shape the minds and influences of women struggling with insecurities, doubts, fears, etc. From this, we created a global movement known as:

Introverted Women Leaders

Introverted Women Leadership is at the forefront of She Rises Studios. Co-CEO and Founder, Adriana Luna Carlos, prides herself on being an innovative and introverted leader.

We, as introverted women, are some of the most sophisticated and creative people on the planet. We don't mind working "quietly" because we excel when we are left to work in the state of mind that we are most comfortable with.

Introverted leaders are great listeners, solution-makers, and trust builders. They show extraordinary confidence in decision-making and team building.

She Rises Studios offers:

- She Rises Studios Publishing
- She Rises Studios Public Relations
- She Rises Studios Podcast
- She Rises Studios Magazine
- Becoming An Unstoppable Woman TV Show
- She Rises Studios Community
- She Rises Studios Academy
- Fenix TV

We won't stop encouraging women to be Unstoppable. This is just the beginning of our global movement.

She Rises, She Leads, She Lives...

With Love,
HANNA OLIVAS
ADRIANA LUNA CARLOS
SHE RISES STUDIOS
www.sherisesstudios.com

Adriana Luna Carlos

Founder & CEO of She Rises Studios
Podcast Host | Best Selling Author | #BAUW Movement Creator

https://www.linkedin.com/company/she-rises-studios/
https://www.instagram.com/sherisesstudios/
https://www.facebook.com/sherisesstudios
www.SheRisesStudios.com

Adriana Luna Carlos is a much sought-after expert in Web and Graphic design as well as a new Podcast Host Personnel for She Rises Studios. For over 10 years she has embraced her passion in the digital arts field along with helping women worldwide overcome their insecure idiosyncrasies. Today, when she's not spending time with her family and friends, you'll often find her helping woman focus on rising up and becoming unafraid of success. To learn more about Adriana Luna Carlos and how she can help you overcome obstacles in your business, mindset, or insecurities, visit www.SheRisesStudios.com.

BREAKING THE STEREOTYPE

By Adriana Luna Carlos

Are you an introverted woman who wants to lead but is held back by common stereotypes? You may have heard that being an introvert puts you at a disadvantage, but that doesn't have to be the case. It's time to move past those misconceptions and free yourself from them!

Being introverted means that a person tends to be more reserved and introspective and prefers solitary activities rather than socializing with others. Introverted individuals may feel drained or overwhelmed by large groups of people or social events and may require time alone to recharge their energy. They may also be more inclined to focus on their internal thoughts, feelings, and experiences than to seek external stimulation.

However, it's important to note that introversion is not the same as shyness or social anxiety. While some introverts may experience shyness or social anxiety, introversion is simply a personality trait that describes how a person interacts with the world around them.

Introverted individuals can be just as outgoing, confident, and booming as extroverted individuals, but they may have a different approach to socializing and decision-making. For example, introverts may prefer to listen more than talk, reflect before acting, and cultivate deep relationships with a few close friends or colleagues rather than an extensive network of acquaintances.

In this chapter, I will be going over ten common stereotypes about introverted women leaders so that you can take control and become the leader you always wanted to be.

Stereotype #1

The first stereotype we'll tackle is the idea that introverts lack confidence. This couldn't be further from the truth – introverts tend to have greater self-awareness and think before they act more than their extroverted counterparts. This means that when it comes time for them to lead a team or make a decision, they can confidently do so, knowing they've thought it through thoroughly.

Stereotype #2

Another stereotype about introverts is that they cannot communicate effectively or build relationships with others. Again, this isn't true – while it may take longer for an introvert to open up and share their thoughts, once they do, they often prove themselves as excellent communicators who can form meaningful connections with others. As leaders, their teams can trust and rely on them for guidance and support.

Stereotype #3

The third stereotype we'll discuss is that introverts are not creative thinkers or problem solvers – but in reality, nothing could be further from the truth! Introverts often bring a unique perspective and view of the world, which helps them come up with creative solutions and outside-the-box ideas which can benefit their teams when it comes time for brainstorming sessions or problem-solving activities.

Stereotypes #4-9

Introverts don't like change;
They don't express emotions;
They are easily overwhelmed;
They don't handle stress well;
They can't take criticism;
They lack ambition -- all false!

In reality, while change may take some getting used to for an introverted leader, once settled into their new environment, they often thrive on being able to make changes as needed. Additionally, while shyness may sometimes prevent an expression of emotion outwardly, inside, there is often a burning passion that allows them to excel at leading teams in times of crisis or adversity. Criticism, too, can help inform decisions made by any leader regardless of personality type - making specific criticisms taken constructively instead of personally will allow any kind of leader to make better decisions in the future.

When it comes to ambition - Introverted Women Leaders have just as much ambition as anyone else - only sometimes it's expressed differently than what society has deemed normal. Taking all this into account shows how individuals such as these should not be held back by preconceived notions about how people should act in terms of personality type but instead given space to thrive based on individual strengths!

Stereotype #10

You Can Tell If Someone Is An Extrovert Or An Introvert By Their Appearance– Definitely not. This one should go without saying; unfortunately, due amount of stereotypes surrounding certain personality types sadly still persists today…. But the truth of the matter is folks cannot accurately judge based solely on looks alone since each unique individual possesses an amazing set of mental and emotional characteristics that help define them as truly set apart from the rest of the pack…

It's clear now that many common stereotypes about Introverted Women Leaders aren't true. These misconceptions hold people back from reaching their full potential when leading teams and making decisions within organizations which needs changing now more than ever before! By busting these myths here today, we hope people will take notice and realize just how important having diverse leadership styles is to ensure everyone gets heard equally, no matter their traits!

The first step toward moving past these misconceptions is recognizing each individual's unique strengths and weaknesses when it comes to leading teams successfully—and understanding how each person contributes differently based on their personal preferences regarding leadership styles/skillsets.

Additionally, embracing yourself in whatever form feels natural is an integral part of developing the potential to become a great leader, whether talkative and outgoing or reserved and quieter. I recommend finding a supportive community, peers, and colleagues, who share similar values and outlooks, which helps ensure long-term success.

Be Your Own Leader: A Mantra for Introverted Women

Introverted women often find themselves in leadership roles where they are expected to lead with confidence and authority. Being an introvert doesn't mean you can't be a great leader! You need to learn how to tap into your inner strength and be your own leader.

One way that introverted women can become better leaders is by embracing their natural personality traits. Introverts tend to be more thoughtful and reflective than extroverts, which can be an asset in a leadership role. Rather than quickly making decisions without considering all of the information available, it pays off for introverts to take their time and consider every angle before concluding. This allows them to make more informed decisions that are better for the team or organization.

Another important aspect of being an introverted leader is learning to communicate effectively with others while maintaining your boundaries. As an introvert, staying quiet during meetings or retreating into yourself when faced with difficult conversations or situations may be tempting. However, this doesn't help anyone if you want your team or organization to succeed—you need to learn how to express yourself clearly yet respectfully so that everyone is on the same page about what needs doing next.

And finally, remember self-care! Being in a leadership role means you will likely face times of stress or anxiety as you try and juggle all sorts of tasks simultaneously. So taking time out for yourself is essential if you want your mind (and body) to function optimally to perform at your best every day. Whether it means scheduling regular breaks throughout the day or finding time each week for some self-care activities like yoga or meditation, ensuring you look after yourself should always remain a top priority as an introverted leader!

When we have the information we need, we can make better decisions. I always want to understand someone's strengths and weaknesses, so I know how to work with them and how they can best work with me. I want to share with you MY strengths and weaknesses from being an introverted individual so that you can either relate or find the difference between yourself as a fellow introvert OR extrovert. Learning about others is always fun!

My Strengths:

1. Good listener: I am a good listener, which is a valuable leadership trait. By listening actively to team members, introverted women leaders can gain insight into their team's needs and challenges and make better-informed decisions.

2. Thoughtful and reflective: I tend to be thoughtful and reflective, which can help me make better decisions. I take time to think through problems and consider multiple perspectives before making decisions, which can lead to better outcomes.

3. Strong focus: I often remain highly focused on my goals and objectives. I stay focused on things other than external factors, which can help me stay on track and achieve my goals.

4. Lead by example: I enjoy leading by example, which can be a powerful leadership style. I may not be the loudest or most charismatic person in the room, but my actions and behaviors can inspire and motivate my team.

My weaknesses:

1. Struggle with public speaking: I often need help with public speaking or presenting in front of large groups. This can be a disadvantage in specific leadership roles where public speaking is required, such as giving presentations to clients or stakeholders. I consciously work on this each time the opportunity arises, and I gradually improve.

2. Need help networking: I also need help with networking, which can be a vital part of building relationships and advancing in specific industries. This can limit opportunities for professional growth and advancement. Because I know this is a weakness of mine, I discuss this with my team and ask for help from others who do not struggle as much. Teamwork makes the dream work.

3. For leadership roles, those who do not know me well or who have not worked with me tend to overlook me for leadership roles because I may need to be more vocal and outgoing than other extroverted within my team or community. This can be frustrating and lead to a lack of representation of introverted women in leadership positions. This is one of the main reasons why this book was created because it is important to know that we DO excel in leadership roles and should not get easily overlooked anymore.

4. I may be perceived as distant: As an introvert, I am often viewed as distant, making it difficult for me to build effective

relationships. This can lead to a lack of trust and cooperation, negatively impacting team dynamics. But the more you become aware of something, the more you can work on things. I constantly do my best to let people know that I am here and care.

Most of these weaknesses mentioned above and some that were not mentioned can be easily overcome by being a good listener.

Builds trust and respect:

By listening to others, a leader demonstrates that they value their opinions, which can build trust and respect. When people feel heard and understood, they are more likely to trust and respect their leader.

- Helps to make better-informed decisions: Leaders who listen to their team members gain valuable insights and perspectives. This can help them make better-informed decisions and avoid potential pitfalls.

- Increases empathy and understanding: Listening can also increase compassion and understanding. When leaders listen to their team members, they better understand their challenges, concerns, and motivations. This can help leaders to be more compassionate and supportive.

- Fosters collaboration and teamwork: When leaders listen to their team members, they create an environment of collaboration and teamwork. Leaders can foster an environment where everyone's contributions are valued by encouraging open communication and active listening.

- Boosts morale and engagement: When leaders listen to their team members, they show they care about their well-being and success. This can boost confidence and engagement, leading to better performance and productivity.

A good listener is a key trait of a good leader because it builds trust and respect, helps make better-informed decisions, increases empathy and understanding, fosters collaboration and teamwork, and boosts morale and engagement.

Overall, being introverted can be a strength and a weakness in a leadership role. The key is to be aware of your strengths and weaknesses and to find ways to leverage your strengths while working on improving your weaknesses.

So there we have it—the mantra for our fellow introverted women leaders: Embrace who you are, communicate effectively, and remember self-care! With these tips in mind, we know that our fellow introverts will make exceptional leaders who inspire those around them with their unique strengths and insights!

Alexis Enterline

The Life Lab
Mindset Coach

https://www.facebook.com/groups/thelifelab/
https://www.instagram.com/alexis.enterline/
https://alexisenterline.com/

Alexis Enterline is a Mindset coach with almost two decades of experience in helping people grow and navigate change. As a Licensed Clinical Social Worker, Alexis understands the importance of self-understanding and uses the latest neuroscience techniques to help women shift their mindset and create the life they want.

Alexis understands that it's not always easy to make changes, but by learning more about how your brain works, you can start making small shifts that will have a big impact down the line.

The Life Lab was created by Alexis as a safe space for women to come together and learn more about themselves. The Life Lab provides tools, guidance, and community to help women succeed. Through monthly support, masterminds, and book clubs a strong sense of self is cultivated and encouraged. Alexis knows that it's not always easy to make changes, but with the right support, anything is possible.

THAT'S A NO FOR ME: THE INTROVERT'S GUIDE TO RECLAIMING TIME AND ENERGY

By Alexis Enterline

I was yearning for a single moment of peace. I constantly criticized myself for repeatedly saying yes to driving friends to soccer games, taking on additional classes, and responsibilities at work when I really wanted to say "no." As I embarked on yet another soccer practice drive, I longed for a week where I could simply relax at home with no obligations. And then March 2020 arrived, and all of those self-imposed pressures vanished.

This sudden turn of events presented me with a rare opportunity to reflect on what truly mattered to me and what I wanted to continue doing. After aligning my priorities with my goals, I discovered the power of saying no with conviction and embracing my newfound freedom.

As an introvert, saying "no" can often feel like a daunting task, but with the right approach, saying "no" to what doesn't serve you can be a liberating experience. I am excited to share my insights and strategies with you so that you, too, can tap into the superpower of no and prioritize your well-being.

Before learning to say "no," it is important to understand the pressure to say "yes."

The pressure for women to say "yes" is rooted in societal expectations and gender norms that view women as nurturing, accommodating, and submissive. This can be especially true for women in leadership positions, who may feel the need to prove themselves and demonstrate their ability to handle multiple responsibilities.

Additionally, women are often expected to prioritize the needs of others before their own, leaving them feeling obligated to say "yes" to requests and invitations, even when they don't want to. This can result in feelings of burnout, resentment, and a lack of personal boundaries.

For introverted women, the pressure to say "yes" can be even greater, as their introspective nature is often misconstrued as passive or accommodating. They may appear to others as easy to push around, making it even more challenging for them to assert their boundaries and prioritize their own needs.

It's important to recognize and challenge these societal expectations and gender norms and to empower women to set healthy boundaries and prioritize their own well-being. Saying "no" is not a sign of weakness but rather a demonstration of strength and self-awareness.

To effectively assert your boundaries and say "no" to requests that don't align with your values and goals, it's crucial to first understand what you're saying "yes" to.

The first step in learning to say "no" is to clarify personal values and goals. This looks like taking time to reflect on what is most important to you and what you want to achieve. Doing this helps prioritize not only your time and energy but also makes it easier to say "no" to requests that don't align with those established values and goals. How do you determine what your values and goals are? You start by reflecting on your values. Write down those values that are most important to you and why they are so meaningful. Some examples might include honesty, creativity, family, or community. Once you are clear on your values, you need to identify your goals. And like you did with your values, write down the goals that you want to achieve in both the short- and long-term. Consider both personal and professional goals, and be specific and realistic. When you are done identifying your most important values and setting your goals, you need to prioritize them. Identify what is most important by ranking them in order of importance. Keep this list in a place where you can see it regularly.

The second step is setting your boundaries. This is done by identifying the types of requests that are the most challenging to say "no" to and setting a clear boundary around them. Boundaries might look like setting aside specific time for work and personal activities or declining invitations that are not aligned with your priorities. You can do this by identifying the challenges by writing down the types of requests that are most challenging to say "no" to. Consider both personal and professional situations. Then you can set the boundary. For each type of request, determine what you need to say "no" to in order to align with your values and goals. Write down these boundaries and be specific about what you will and will not do. Keep this list in a place where you can see it regularly and stick to it.

The third step in learning to say "no" is to practice self-care. Make sure you are taking care of yourself and prioritizing your own well-being. This might mean saying "no" to requests that are too demanding or stressful or taking time for yourself to recharge and refocus. There are many ways you can practice self-care nowadays. Here are just a few that I suggest:

- Identify stressors: Write down the activities or situations that are most stressful for you and consider why they are stressful.

- Plan for self-care: For each stressor, write down what you can do to take care of yourself and prioritize your well-being. Consider things like exercise, meditation, or spending time with loved ones.

- Seek support: Surround yourself with supportive people who understand and respect your boundaries. This might mean seeking out a mentor, joining a supportive community, or talking to a friend or family member about your goals and priorities. Your supportive people might change as time goes by. For this moment in time, identify supportive individuals: Write down the people in your life who understand and respect your boundaries. Consider family members, friends, mentors, or community members. For each of these individuals, write down how you can seek their support, whether that's through regular check-ins, asking for advice, or simply having someone to talk to.

- Re-evaluate regularly: Regularly take time to re-evaluate your values, goals, and priorities and make any necessary adjustments. This will help you stay aligned with what you really want to do and make it easier to say "no" to requests that don't serve you.

- Schedule regular check-ins: Write down a schedule for regularly re-evaluating your values, goals, and priorities, and adjusting your boundaries and self-care practices as needed. This could be monthly, quarterly, or annually, depending on your needs.

- Reflect on your progress: During each check-in, reflect on your progress and consider what is working well and what could be improved. Make any necessary adjustments, and be proud of your achievements and progress.

As introverts, we often face unique challenges when asserting our boundaries and saying "no." We may worry about causing conflict, disappointing others, or missing out on opportunities. However, learning to say "no" is a crucial aspect of taking care of ourselves and maintaining a healthy and fulfilling life. In this section, I will share the strategies and techniques I use for saying "no" in a confident and empowering way.

One of the most congruent strategies I have discovered for saying "no" is the application of the "positive no."

The "positive no" is a communication technique that was first introduced by William Ury, co-founder of the Harvard Program on Negotiation. The "positive no" offers a way to decline requests in a positive, assertive, and respectful manner without causing conflict or offense.

The "positive no" starts with acknowledging the request and expressing appreciation for the person making it. Then, instead of immediately saying "no," the focus is on highlighting your own positive priorities and why they are meaningful to you. The "no" is then communicated in a clear and direct manner, expressing regret if necessary, and ending with a positive statement or offer of support.

The "positive no" is a helpful alternative to the traditional "no" because it reduces the potential for conflict and offense and helps to maintain positive relationships. It also allows you to assert your boundaries and priorities in a confident and respectful manner while still demonstrating empathy and consideration for others.

Let me give you a real-life example:

In the past, I was approached by a friend to attend a networking event on one of my most sacred personal care days, F**k Around Friday. A day dedicated to my own wellbeing. Past Lexy would feel the pressure to attend and not let her friend down even though it conflicted with the one day a month put aside for her.

Using the "positive no" looks like this:

I am so excited for your event! It is amazing that you are doing that! Thank you so much for thinking of me; however, I am committed to taking some time for myself that day. I would love to let some of my friends know about it, though!

By using the "positive no," I can assert my boundaries, prioritize my well-being, stay aligned with my belief that I do not break promises to myself, and maintain a positive relationship with my friend. I am also demonstrating the importance of personal well-being and positively setting boundaries.

Another strategy I have used successfully is taking a step back and evaluating the impact a "yes" will have on my life.

It's important for me to recognize that saying "yes" to something can have far-reaching effects on my life. By taking the time to assess the true cost of saying "yes," I can make decisions that are in line with my personal values and goals. This includes considering the amount of time and effort required, as well as any potential indirect costs such as increased stress levels, burnout, or neglect of other important responsibilities.

For example, as a woman leader faced with a new project proposal, it's essential to assess its impact on my existing responsibilities and workload. If I'm feeling overextended and burdened, declining the offer or proposing to delay it until a more suitable time may be the most suitable option. However, if the project aligns with my personal and professional aspirations, it may be worth taking on, even if it requires additional effort in the short term.

Ultimately, the true cost of saying "yes" is about making choices that prioritize my well-being and ensure that I have the energy and resources to pursue my passions and goals. By being honest with myself about what I can realistically handle, I can avoid feeling overwhelmed and stressed and maintain a healthy balance in my life.

Think of yourself as an air traffic controller managing the flow of demands and requests that come your way. You are the only one who understands and knows about all of the demands on your time, and you stand at the center of all the requests that come your way.

It's time to take control of your time and prioritize tasks and responsibilities in an organized and effective manner. You have the power to direct and manage the demands on your time, making decisions about what tasks to tackle first and how to allocate your time most effectively. Take ownership of your time and recognize that you are the only one who truly knows your priorities, what you need to get done, and how best to allocate your time.

By becoming the air traffic controller of your time, you can make the most of your time, spending it on the things that matter most to you. You'll find yourself more productive, reaching your goals, and leading a more fulfilling and balanced life.

To put it simply, asserting oneself and saying "no" is a demonstration of strength and empowerment, especially for introverts who understand the importance of self-care and boundary-setting. Assert your right to live on your terms by staying true to personal needs, embracing individuality, and never compromising your well-being for the sake of others. The next time you receive an invitation or request that does not align with your values and goals, stand tall and confidently say "no." Your peace of mind and happiness are a testament to your courage and self-assuredness.

The art of saying "no" has revolutionized my life in the most profound and empowering ways. For years, I felt trapped in a cycle of constant compromise, sacrificing my values and personal goals to meet the expectations of others. However, by embracing the power of boundary-setting and self-care, I was finally able to break free from that cycle and reclaim my life.

The freedom I have gained by saying "no" has allowed me to pursue my lifelong dream of starting my own business, and it has given me the opportunity to embrace my individuality as an introvert. I have learned to value my alone time and not apologize for my unique needs and preferences. This newfound sense of control has allowed me to deepen my relationships with my family and align my actions with my values and goals.

Saying "no" has also been a transformative journey of self-discovery. I have become more self-aware and fallen in love with myself for the first time in my life. No longer burdened by the need to constantly please others, I can stand tall and live my life on my own terms, unapologetically and with grace.

I want to share this empowering message with you, too. The ability to say "no" is a gift that can bring immense positive changes to your life. By embracing self-care and boundary-setting, you can reclaim your life, pursue your passions, and live with purpose and joy. So go ahead, take control, and say "no" to the things that do not serve your highest good. Your happiness and well-being are worth it. If it's a no for me, it can be a no for you, too.

For more resources on embracing your introverted superpowers visit: alexisenterline.com/bookbonus

Michelle Bell

CEO of Virtual Work Wife

https://www.linkedin.com/company/virtual-work-wife
https://www.facebook.com/Virtual-Work-Wife
https://www.instagram.com/virtualworkwife/
www.virtualworkwife.com
www.healthbossinstitute.com

Michelle Bell is the CEO of Virtual Work Wife, a Marketing Agency that is anything but typical.

With a specialty in workflow and process automation, our agency provides personalized solutions for any size business seeking to create more balance.

Founded to help busy entrepreneurs like herself find creative solutions so they could work around their family schedule rather than scheduling family around work, our core values are:

Work less - Make more - Do the things you love

By focusing on strategic solutions, wholistically balanced campaigns, and the belief that authentic marketing will always win over formulas, the Agency provides a one-stop-shop for client care and jobs where talent is fostered, and growth is encouraged.

Lifting people up into their own success stories is what gets me out of bed in the morning. Being of service and surrounding yourself with clients and friends who share in your core values is the true measure of accomplishment.

I'M AN INTROVERT.
WHAT'S YOUR SUPERPOWER?

By Michelle Bell

"I'm sorry if I seem uninterested
Or I'm not listenin' or I'm indifferent
Truly, I ain't got no business here
But since my friends are here, I just came to kick it
But really I would rather be at home all by myself not in this room."
—Alessia Cara

Girlfriend really hit it on the head when she wrote those lyrics. If this isn't the anthem of the introverted, I just don't know what is.

Hi, my name is Michelle, and I'm an introverted leader.

That's super easy to say in writing. To say in person… not so much. But I'm working on it. Every. Single. Day.

Because I'm also an extrovert.

Crazy right? But you can be both things. Finding the balance is where it's at. So what's a girlboss to do? I want the spotlight. I want to be the headliner. I just feel like swallowing my tongue for the first 2-3 minutes every time I take the stage.

Every Time.

Like seriously, why is it so hard to introduce myself? I've been Michelle for 50+ years but *actually saying,* "Hi I'm Michelle" feels more painful than those times I pushed a bowling ball out my coozie.

By the way, Michelle today is a total badass, but Michelle 1.0? That one was a hot mess!

As a kid, we moved a lot, and I never created attachments to people. Circumstances produced in me a learned shyness that took years to overcome. On the inside, I was this total overachiever who always wanted to win, but on the outside, I struggled to interact within a group setting. It was overwhelming and would often take several days and lots of naps to recover from.

Things didn't get any better in my teens when I moved in with my dad. I mean we weren't moving every other month anymore, but being a teen in the 80s living in a small town didn't leave much room for grace. Back then, people simply labeled you a weirdo, and that was that. There was no acceptance or tolerance. Those are Millennial terms.

Still, I tried to blend in. I joined sports and clubs, and I tried to overcome my "shyness" and be like everyone else. Like, all the other girls made it look so easy. They seemed to bask in the energy of others and never got tired of being a part of the crowd.

Meanwhile, I would get tired and cranky for what seemed like no reason at all. I felt like crawling out of my skin all the time and would often separate from the crowd. I wasn't trying to be rude but was often told I was being anti-social or bitchy. I felt broken. I *believed* I was the weirdo they said I was.

No matter how hard I tried, I couldn't shake what I now know was my introverted tendencies, and I resented myself for it. I wanted to be the team captain, I knew I had the right stuff, but I couldn't express what I wanted in a group setting. I blamed my "shyness" for keeping me from being chosen.

That belief stuck with me for years. So much so that when I entered the workforce, I thought that if I wanted to be a leader, I had to be outgoing and loud like those other girls. Little did I know how very wrong I was!

Corporate Life (or the lack thereof)

Meetings, managers, and office politics, oh my! If I thought high school was hard, it was nothing compared to working for a Fortune 500!

To say my foray into the corporate world was a disaster is a complete understatement. Introverted nature aside, some people just aren't meant to work for *the man*.

It's me. I'm some people!

So what's a poor introverted mama with conformity issues to do? Start my own business, of course!

 Side note: if you want to know more about that story, get my book Dream Big, Do Bigger www.virtualworkwife.com/

Turns out, running a virtual business and raising kids created this beautiful armor for me to hide behind. For years I met with clients and employees one on one via Skype or Zoom. It was absolute bliss. And hey, if things got too overwhelming, there was literally a built-in escape plan…

Oops the internet died.
Sorry, I can't travel for meetings, I have kids.

My business and my kids grew, and life was good. But it was a slow boil. Over time, my bubble got smaller and smaller. Without realizing it, I was becoming more isolated. But I was completely happy In my self-imposed confinement.

I got real good at hiding my introversion. So good, in fact, that I co-founded a second business and started running live group training courses. It wasn't like the people were really "there." I didn't even need to have my camera on, so it wasn't like they could see me. My extroverted side was getting to come out and play without the stress of being with people in a real setting.

It was the best of both worlds.

Most people who met me wouldn't automatically think "Oh she's an introvert," but they didn't know how much effort it took for me to leave the house. They don't know how draining it was to be "on" or how much time it took for me to recover.

Not even my family knew how easy it was to let my introverted nature keep me isolated. It was over a decade before I was forced to take a crash course in interacting with the real world again; during the time when literally everyone else was hiding from it!

Enter the Spicy Flu Era.

After 14 years of working at home in virtual solitude, my bubble burst. With the stay-at-home order in place thanks to the rona, my daughter came home from college. My husband's job closed, and my youngest was now homeschooling. The outside world was *inside my bubble!*

I was overwhelmed. The sensory overload was unbearable. *I was unbearable!* And I had no idea why. Top it off with a healthy portion of guilt for being unhappy my family was home, and yeah life was sucky.

I started doing research into depression and anxiety. I mean, it's not normal to want to send your family packing in the middle of a pandemic, right?!?

That's when I stumbled across an online quiz – *Are You an Introvert or Extrovert?* Let me tell you, all the lightbulbs went off. I finally had an explanation for why I was the way I was. I learned what being an extrovert or introvert really meant.

For the first time, I felt like I understood myself. My introversion was actually a strength. Knowing and accepting that gave me a whole new perspective on being a better leader in my businesses, community, and family.

When Opportunity Knocks

So there I was, feeling like I truly understood myself for the first time in my life, when something happened that completely changed my trajectory.

While I'd been working from home for decades, most people were struggling to figure out how to do it. They were looking for help navigating the transition from brick and mortar businesses to the online marketplace. and they were looking to me for advice. I was getting requests to speak on virtual summits and live webinars at a rate I could barely keep up with. And I had this newfound confidence in myself. I was learning to use my introverted nature to my advantage.

But you know what they say, God gives his silliest battles to his funniest clowns. No wait, that's not it. Ahem… He gives his toughest battles to his strongest soldiers. Yeah, that's the one.

So, DoD puts the toughest battle right in my lap. Three speaking engagements live at a 5-day conference, in another state, with an expected 2-3 thousand attendees! Not only would I have to stand on a stage, I'd have to travel to get there. Yikes!

But as Gene Hackman said in The Replacements, winners always want the ball. So, of course, I said yes. Did it go according to plan? Nope. Not even close.

Turns out I have a near pathological fear of falling off the stage. Don't judge, some of us weren't born with perfect spatial awareness. Or any at all in my case. But the key to success in any situation is learning to adapt and overcome. The only easy day was yesterday.

So, after we all had a good laugh at my expense, the tech nerds moved the equipment off the stage to the floor so I could feel more secure. I spoke up for myself and what I needed to feel safe and provide value to the audience. It was an amazing event that was just the first step on an incredible journey towards where we are today.

What I've Learned Along The Way

At this point, I've learned that being shy and being introverted are not the same thing, and there are varying degrees of being an introvert. Everyone has a little bit of both introvert and extrovert inside them. Sometimes it's easier for me to act like an extrovert but it takes a lot of downtime for me to recharge. Knowing that helps me plan out my events and manage my stress levels.

There seems to be this idea that being an introvert means not liking people.
While that might be true for some, it's not a foregone conclusion. It isn't a matter of liking or not liking people. It's more about managing your reserves. Being around too many people for too long can be overstimulating and draining. Just like some people get hangry when they don't eat, introverts get tiranxious when they are peopled out.

Many speculate that between 15 and 50 percent of people are introverts. That might explain why being an introvert is often misunderstood. The majority of the populace views the world from an entirely different perspective—an extroverted one. It's easy to see why they might think their view is better.

But God doesn't make mistakes. He made both introverts and extroverts for a reason. As an introvert, you are beautiful and kind and you have an affinity for deep conversation and strong, lasting connections. These are excellent skills for a business owner, community leader, guardian, or friend.

Acceptance

Knowing and loving all the parts of yourself is a pretty huge step on the path of adulthood. Not gonna lie, I'm not there 100% of the time, but I have learned to love my introverted nature. I can be loud and silly and funny and fire up a crowd, but I also give myself the grace to take a day off after an event and decompress.

I am a better boss and consultant when I acknowledge my introversion. I've learned to delegate some of the handholding tasks. I get less drained when I can arrive as the guest star versus being the hype man and the headliner. And let's not forget, effective delegation is a hallmark of a great leader!

Tips for Living the Introvert Life

Identify Your Perfect Fuel Mix

Okay yes, I'm married to a grease monkey. He taught me that the right mix of gas and oil is what makes a motor run. So what's your mix?

It's important to know what you need and even more so to ensure you get it. All too often we let our own needs take a backseat to clients, employees, or family, but you can't drive on E forever (trust me, I've tried), so make sure you take the time to refill your tank.

Do you need a quiet night at home with the fam? Or an afternoon on the porch swing with a good book? Maybe you need a nap or three, like I do. Or maybe you just need to Netflix and chill to get your motor running again.

People Might Find it Hard to Get to Know You

Some people might see your quiet demeanor as distant or unfriendly, which means you might have to take the initiative to start conversations with others. Ask open-ended questions that encourage the other person to share more about themselves.

Introverts are great listeners, so put that superpower to good use! Once you get the ball rolling, the other person can carry the conversation, taking the pressure off of you. Building relationships is worthwhile work, but remember to have patience with yourself and take breaks when needed.

Know Your Boundaries

My kids taught me a valuable lesson in setting boundaries with my clients. I have work time and I have family time, and never the two should cross. What took a while to learn, though, was setting my own boundaries and respecting what my introversion needs for me to be productive.

If I'm scheduled to travel or speak at an onsite event, it's important for my mental health that I block out a day or two before the event. I need this time to get mentally and physically ready without having the added stress of juggling clients and family at the same time.

After the event, I block at least one day to decompress and recharge. I'm not any good to my clients or family if I'm still overstimulated or tiranxious.

These blackout dates are just as important as the events themselves. It's become a normal and necessary addition to my schedule. The right clients understand that for me to be 100% there for them, I also need to be honoring myself.

Just Because You Can Doesn't Mean You Should

Emotional energy has a cost, and you need to decide if you're willing to pay the price. Even that trip to Starbies with a girlfriend can be overwhelming if you do it the same day as a big client meeting.

Remember that 3-day event I mentioned earlier? I told you it didn't go as planned. I should have told them three talks in 5 days was too many.

I should have respected my boundaries, but I was jazzed, and well, you know, winners always want the ball.

But if you're not giving yourself enough recovery time between social outings, you might not be the only one that suffers. Your girlfriend might not understand why you're being tiranxous. Your client might not get the best of you, which could lead to financial loss.

When you're presented with an opportunity, large or small, respect your calendar and remember to weigh the emotional energy cost before you commit.

Take a Warm Up Lap

Something I find really helpful when faced with a large group or meeting is taking a warm up lap. I'll find one or two people around the room and give them a quick hint at what I've planned to discuss. It's my way of easing into talking to the bigger crowd.

It's purely for personal gain. I get a chance to hear myself talking and gauge reactions. Plus, when you make a personal connection it doesn't feel like talking to strangers anymore and it gives you someone to make eye contact with later on if you start to feel overwhelmed.

Don't Ignore Your Warning Lights

Yes, it's another car reference, don't act so surprised. ☺

Every human has their own set of warning lights. Do you know what yours are?

- Do you get easily irritated by that chick with the loud laugh?

- Does the sound of Darrel's constant throat clearing make you want to scream?

- Is that corner at the back of the room calling your name?

- Do you feel compelled to find the nearest bathroom and hide?

These are warning lights. They're trying to tell you it's time to take a break before you break down. Ignore these signals at your peril!

Look I get it, you're a superhero boss mom warrior queen, but even you need a break once in a while. It's okay to step away from the crowd. It's okay to ask your employee to field questions for a minute or have your spouse take over the conversation with Miss Sally after Sunday service. What's not okay is ignoring the warning that something is draining you.

Personally, I don't do breakfast networking meetings. I want to, cuz hello breakfast, but it's just not in the cards for me. I am all for networking and getting to know other business owners, but I've learned that the constant sound of silverware clanking against plates and coffee cups is like nails on a chalkboard. Forget tiranxious, that's a one-way trip to homicidal!

Being an Introvert is NOT a Limitation!

You can totally enjoy socializing and still be an introvert. If Oprah and Meryl can survive Hollywood as self-proclaimed introverts, I'm pretty sure we can handle the occasional PTA meeting or company Christmas party!

Being an introvert doesn't mean avoiding social gatherings, it simply means finding ways to make it work for you. Like spending time with one or two good friends instead of mingling with a larger crowd. The key thing to remember is to honor your need for some downtime later on.

Stacey Dorenfeld

Hadassah, the Women's Zionist Organization of America, Inc. National Advocacy Leader

https://www.linkedin.com/in/stacey-dorenfeld-352243141/
https://www.facebook.com/staceydorenfeld
www.dorenfeldlaw.com
www.staceyinsideout.com

I live the life I have because of the people and experiences I've been blessed with.

I currently am on the National Grassroots Advocacy team for Hadassah, The Women's Zionist Organization of America. In that capacity, I advocate with Federal and State Representatives to expand human rights. I often speak and hold workshops about domestic advocacy.

I'm passionate about making the world a better placc for the next generation, which has included spearheading the passage of critical legislation to help victims of human trafficking.

I am passionate about improving our experience as humans; which includes fighting antisemitism, securing sane gun laws and championing women's rights.

I received my degree in communications. I'm an entrepreneur at heart; creating an original line of motivational jewelry.

I work as the Operations Manager for our family law firm. I am a published author of four books, and the face behind the lifestyle blog, www.StaceyInsideOut.com.

YOU'VE GOT TO BE KIDDING ME!

By Stacey Dorenfeld

When the publisher asked me to write a chapter for this book about being an introverted leader, my first impulse was to say no. I wondered if I could call myself an introvert because if you knew me, you would think I was an extrovert. I am talkative and, at times, even over-the-top silly. But, after researching and looking at myself, I realized I am an introverted extrovert. If I could make up a name for this syndrome, it would be "bi-vertism." So, about a decade ago, when a friend suggested that I apply for a leadership program, you can understand why I blurted out, "You've got to be kidding me; I'm not a leader!" I can't imagine those words coming out of me now. Presently, with a load of doubt, curiosity, and determination, I have stepped into the role of a leader.

It now seems obvious that I was meant to be a leader. But it certainly took a while for the idea to sink in. After all, my inner critic was screaming loud and clear, "You're not a leader! You weren't even a line leader in school." How the insecurities came and settled inside doesn't matter. I was a 50-plus-year-old woman, and things were about to change.

Deciding to participate in leadership is not the same as being a leader. For many years, I had been leading in my quiet way in creating bracelets, doing design work, writing children's books, and running my family business. I have always been my extended family's go-to person for guidance and advice, and friends have always reached out to me for comfort and support. In these ways, I have been leading for quite some time, but it was only when the invitation to participate in a formal leadership program did I ever think that I had what it took to be a leader.

I have had several occasions where I could have taken on more leadership roles, but I needed more confidence to accept those responsibilities. My first opportunity came as a new member of Hadassah, the Women's Zionist Organization of America. My passion for having a voice led me to inquire about a leadership program. The Executive Director had a confidence in me that I did not. "Stacey, you absolutely are a leader," she said when I asked if I had what it took. The mere thought of applying for a leadership program with a national organization of over 300,000 women terrified me. I had recently begun to do uncomfortable things to grow beyond my self-imposed limitations, and applying to be a Hadassah Leadership Fellow was spot on.

But soon after, the real battle began. "Stop procrastinating," I told myself as I stared intently at the blank form. I nearly choked when asked about my past experience, leadership activities, and the most important question of all, "What makes me a leader?" Me, I was just a mom. I was just Stacey, slowly coming out of my shell after living most of my life like a turtle, afraid to stick my neck out into the world. Then I began thinking back. I remember being on the board of our local synagogue and even a Girl Scout leader. "Whoop-de-doo for me," I whispered as I chewed on my pen.

Around the same time, the woman who ran the Jewish Women's Initiative asked me to lead a women's trip to Israel. "Are you sure you want me to do this?" I questioned her judgment. "Of course," she said, "you have just what it takes to lead the group." It was scary, but having this woman believe in me gave me the confidence and courage to say yes to leading this life-altering trip. It was only a short time before I began interviewing the candidates, designing the itinerary, preparing the agenda, and planning a few lessons. It is interesting how my leadership skills kicked in without me giving it much thought. But I itched with self-doubt, and that nagging itch would not go away, no matter how hard I scratched.

Growing up, I didn't have parents instilling confidence in me, so—as with most things in life—I had to figure it out on my own. I spent most of my time alone, overly passive, and highly reserved. Early on, I struggled with math so much that I would cry after every test. I painfully waited for the results that were usually marked with a big, fat "D." I was already doing extra credit homework. When I was learning long division, Mr. Paschal, my fifth-grade math teacher, got so frustrated he threw an eraser at my head. No matter how hard I tried, the math made no sense. "You're not smart, Stacey; you didn't get your father's brain," my mother said to me when I came home in tears with chalk dust in my hair. I wanted to fight back by telling her she was wrong, but instead, I stayed quiet and bit my tongue until I could taste the blood. I had no voice.

Between childhood and what I like to think of as self-actualization, I moved to New York, started a few companies, designed houses, and wrote; from the outside, I probably appeared accomplished and together, but inside, I was still that kid with chalk in her hair.

When you are told you aren't smart or good enough to go to college, you have a choice: either believe the lie and let that belief drive you to fail or let the lie propel you to succeed. For me, the pensive, introverted Stacey had some deep-rooted, innate determination that told me I could go to college, and that determination was not a lie. Succeeding would be another story. At the time, I chalked up studying and graduating with honors as a simple rebellion against my mother and father, who had told me I would fail. I was going to show them both that they were wrong about me. In reality, not only did I show them, but I also showed myself what it takes to succeed. I didn't know this then; I was only reacting to circumstances.

Like every strong, introverted leader, productively channeling your inner voice is vital to the role. I constantly ask myself, "Stacey, is what you are telling yourself true? Or is the old lie about being dumb and inadequate rearing its ugly head?" I have slowly turned those negative thoughts into motivation by challenging and analyzing my long-held assumptions.

Learning to silence my inner critic and embrace my true leadership potential has been challenging and, at times, terrifying. I have had to constantly battle my doubts and insecurities to open myself up to being a leader. I realize that my inner critic can be a powerful tool, but if left unchecked, it will be my most crippling enemy. I have to remember that I can choose how I think and act. But I must admit, since I've been like a turtle, change has come slowly. Hiding behind my smile, dressing the part, and acting as if I am secure and confident is something I excel at. Just like the inner critic, that is not me either. I am a mix of open and closed, rise and fall, good and bad. This realization has allowed me to lead because I now know I am but a human on a human journey.

Recognizing myself as a leader forced me to think differently about who I am. Everything damaging I felt about myself slowly eroded as I opened up to new experiences. I was accepted into the Hadassah Leadership program, and before I knew it, I was leading a successful trip to Israel for the Jewish Women's Initiative. It happened so fast I did not have time to focus on my fear, and I had to embrace my shyness. I kept asking myself how I was doing what I was doing. It was so far from my nature. I didn't know. I just did what felt right, and I let myself be. There was no parrot on my shoulder telling me I could not do something and no one to stop me from pursuing a passion that fueled my soul.

Soon, this national organization entrusted me to call on Federal and State legislators and meet with them to discuss Hadassah's legislative priorities. I came up with an idea for a bill that would help victims of human trafficking that eventually became law. I taught other women to use their voices to effect positive change. Making a difference tasted sweet, starkly contrasting the metallic taste in my mouth when I was forced to bite my tongue. However, as empowered as I was, I could not help but feel vulnerable, like an imposter. I imagined everyone could see through me. I struggled to keep up the pretense of a poised, confident woman. I was in a leadership position, but when I looked in the mirror, I saw someone who was inadequate and sure to fail. That was the lie I was telling myself and the lie I had to squash before it was too late. I was a leader, and it was okay to be scared and shy. No one seemed to notice; if they did, they did not seem to care. They just wanted more of what I seemed to offer – my passion for advocacy, my desire to end human trafficking, and my fight for women's health equity.

I had to get used to being referred to as a leader, and I still struggle with it all. At first, the title did not seem to fit. But it did not matter if I felt shy about making speeches or uptight in meetings because I was doing something that made me feel alive. I had a fierce determination to make a difference. With time, I learned to accept that I was not perfect and that it was alright. I worked hard and cared about the work I did. I gained the trust of those around me and found my footing as a leader.

I have learned that being a leader requires time, commitment, and steadiness, but most of all, it takes trusting your gut. Learning to trust yourself takes time, self-awareness, and confidence. I did not realize it when it happened, but I learned to trust my gut. It never lies. Deep inside, I knew I was not what my parents saw; the introverted leader others saw in me was hidden behind the baggage of my childhood.

As an introvert, it never dawned on me to purposely put myself in the leadership role. It wasn't easy at first. Other people's experiences and perceived intelligence made me cautious and tentative. By letting my gut lead instead of my head, I became more confident about my decision-making skills and relationships. Trusting my gut is scary, and it requires courage and resilience. It also permits me not to be perfect. A good leader is not perfect, and she is fearless in admitting it. Ah, what a relief that is.

A good leader is a good listener. As an advocate, I needed to show the women I was leading that I heard them when they expressed confusion over a bill's text or fears about meeting with their legislators. I needed to listen to them when their ideas were better than mine. I remembered the pain I experienced as a child of having no voice, and I used it to become a good listener. Everyone has value, and every idea is worth exploring. It takes patience and confidence to be quiet and allow ideas to mature organically. Being a good listener has given me the gift of ideas I never imagined.

As a self-critic, I overthink everything. This habit has not always worked, but with time, I have learned to allow myself the gift of slowing down, looking around me, listening to my body, and feeding on the energy of others. In this journey, I have learned that being a leader is not about the leader but about those you lead. I do for others, not for me. Not that I do not get satisfaction, I do. Knowing that people are listening and being motivated to push themselves for more is fuel enough to climb above my self-doubt, past, and fear of the future and climb and rise.

I love the quote by Louis Pasteur, "Where observation is concerned, chance favors the prepared mind." The importance of self-observation cannot be underestimated. Embracing the leader I have come to be has taught me to take time to observe myself before I go out into the world. Where am I? What am I feeling? Am I grounded? Am I in line with my gut? Moments of self-reflection give me great confidence to walk into a room with a group of women and present a proposal to a senator or speak in front of a large audience. A passion for standing up for human rights guides me in leading the women around me. We all have the same vision: to better our world for ourselves and future generations. I genuinely care about the policies I am advocating for and am interested in every woman on this journey with me. When I step back and take the temperature of a room or those around me, I know I am actively leading. I genuinely care about what I do, who I do it with, and who I do it for.

My search for inner peace has guided me throughout my life. I have had to be resilient and patient and learn acceptance. I have had to get to know myself every day because I constantly evolve. It is about who my soul is at this very moment. And right now, my soul says I am to be a mom, a business operator, an entrepreneur, a writer, and a leader for an organization near and dear to my heart.

In the grand scheme of things, you can become a leader at any age, and if you step into yourself rather than away from yourself, you may find you too are a leader, introverted or not. And, yes, I may sometimes still be uncertain and intimidated by the challenges ahead of me, but I have actively faced my fears and moved forward. I have dedicated my time, resources, and energy to teaching other women to use their voices by advocating for issues to better humanity because I know how good it feels to be part of the change. A good leader is a work in progress like I am. So, I embrace every opportunity for learning and growth that comes my way and take solace in the fact that I am not alone on this journey, or, shall I say, this fantastic obstacle course called life!

Angela Bell

The Inspired & Profitable Mompreneur
Mompreneur Success Coach and Women's Wealth Advocate

https://www.linkedin.com/in/angela-bell-776a529/
https://www.facebook.com/angela.bell.3597
https://www.instagram.com/i.am.angelabell/
https://www.inspirednprofitablemompreneur.com/

Angela Bell is the founder of The Mom Magic Anthology Series and the Mom Magic Movement! She is also the founder and CEO at The Inspired & Profitable Mompreneur Business, Podcast, Magazine & TV Show.

Angela is on a mission to empower moms around the world to stand in their power, embrace their dreams, and create their own business! Angela is a multi-passionate entrepreneur, business coach for moms, and mom of twins.

She has built multiple 6 & 7 figure business, published several books, and helped hundreds of women launch and grow their own Inspired & Profitable online businesses. Angela is committed to helping other moms live their very best lives on their own terms!

CREATING AND LEADING FROM A QUIET PLACE

By Angela Bell

I enjoy silence. In fact, I often search for it.

I find it funny how uncomfortable silence can make people. I'm the opposite; idle chit chat makes me uncomfortable. Loud noises and crowds make me uncomfortable. Too much noise makes it hard for me to hear my inner voice that speaks with universal wisdom.

My name is Angela, and I am what you'd call an empath and an introvert. Most people who know me well don't think I'm an introvert, but that's just because I'm comfortable with them. I chose my circle carefully.

It took me a long time to accept my introversion and see it as a strength. I spent a lot of my life trying to learn to be loud, how to assert myself, call attention to myself, and control the conversation. But it always felt wrong and left me feeling drained.

Don't get me wrong, I love the spotlight when I feel called to take it. And I love to speak, share, and lead. I just like to do it in my own way and in my own time.

My way of being runs contrary to the noise and business of today. Everyone is yelling to be heard, forcing things to go their way, and asserting dominance and judgment over others. To be honest, I don't understand why they are exerting all that effort when there is a much easier way.

As I have begun to embrace my way of being and doing, I have found it has its own unique strengths and advantages. It feels better to me, it creates an environment of peace, and accomplishes my daily goal to add more love and joy to the world.

Six key aspects of my personal style of leadership are:

- Invite don't force.
- Listen to hear and learn, not to respond.
- If a solution is not win/win, everyone loses.
- I am not better or worse than anyone, just different.
- Remember, everyone has something to offer and something to teach you.
- My way is not the only way, nor is anyone else's.

Invite, Don't Force

Albert Einstein is quoted as saying, "Peace cannot be kept by force; it can only be achieved by understanding." I believe this quote can be applied universally. It has been shown that what we resist persists. When we try to force people or things to bend to our will, we are met with resistance. Whether this is regarding a world view, a task to be completed at the office, or with our children, when we try to force things to happen, we are met with equal and opposite resistance.

I have lived my years of trying to force things. I tried to force success, force relationships to work, and force people to accept me, and all I got for it was frustration and crap self-esteem.

When we invite, open the door and say "hey, come check this out," we are saying nothing about the rightness or wrongness of what currently exists, and therefore, we are met with no resistance. Instead, we provoke curiosity and open up the lines for creative thinking. We create space for people to have their thoughts and opinions and invite them to change their minds. In short, it feels better, so it's easier.

Listen to Hear and Learn, Not Respond

You can learn so much if you just listen. When I enter a new environment, I am often the quietest person in the room. It's not that

I don't have anything to say. It's just that I prefer to listen and observe. You can learn a lot about people and situations when you just listen. People's actions and ways of interacting will tell you more about them than their words. And if you listen intently enough, you can see the humanity in even the most abrasive person.

In today's society, everyone is so busy trying to be seen and heard that no one is seeing or hearing. We are desperately seeking someone, anyone to acknowledge us and see us for who we really are. Most people are so busy preparing their response that they never get around to hearing what the person in front of them is actually trying to say. Which is often "I'm here, I want to be seen. I want to be known and understood." I have found that the easiest way to become the most popular person in the room is to actively listen to people. While that is never my purpose, it's just a positive outcome.

I actually enjoy listening to people. I value their thoughts, experiences, and opinions, even if they differ from my own.

If a Solution is not Win/Win, Everyone Loses

My Dad always told me to look for a win/win solution. This idea has always felt right to me. I have never been comfortable achieving or obtaining things if it was at someone else's expense.

I guess that's why the whole concept of competition rubs me the wrong way. It implies that for one person to win, another must lose. For one person to have, another must have not.

If we win at the expense of another, we have essentially made ourselves more important than them. Our wants and needs must be met at all costs. If anything, it shows the world our fears and insecurities, not our power and importance.

Finding a win/win solution isn't always the easiest way, nor is it the fastest way. It takes time, effort, and care. We have to be willing to listen to what the other party needs and why it matters to them. We have to value their needs as much as our own.

When we invest in finding win/win solutions, we invest in ourselves, our community, our teams, and our business. We do the work to benefit more than just ourselves. We add to the world instead of taking from it. And everyone benefits.

I am not Better or Worse than Anyone, Just Different

Comparison is a constant in today's society. Everyone is looking at everyone else and measuring.

I compared myself to other people for years, never quite measuring up. Like I said, I have always been quiet. I have always liked what I liked, not what was popular. This led to a lot of instances where I felt like I wasn't good enough, which lead to shame.

It wasn't until I came to appreciate my uniqueness that I could let go of the shame. Once I stopped trying to be like everyone else and stopped trying to be accepted, I was able to accept myself. The funny part is, the more I accepted other people as they were, without trying to change them or wishing they were different, the easier it became to accept myself. It's cyclical. When we love and accept ourselves, flaws and all, we can better love and accept others. When we realize that our differences make the world exciting, we stop trying to fit in and force others into a mold.

I will never ask someone to do something, in business or otherwise, that I am not willing to do myself. I do not think I am better or worse than anyone else. I am just uniquely me.

This experience made me very aware of how other people feel. I know what it's like to feel less than, so I work very hard to ensure I don't make people feel that way. Which leads to a very important point…

Everyone Has Something to Offer or Teach You

And yes, I mean EVERYONE. Even the person that drives you the craziest.

When we look for the good in people or the lesson from a situation, we reframe how we see the world. Instead of seeing "bad" we see interesting. Instead of seeing problems, we see questions. When we are willing to look for the good in people and what they have to offer, we make space for them to showcase their unique skills.

It's so easy to judge and write people off. It takes effort to give people time to shine. One of the gifts of being introverted is that I don't talk to fill space. This creates an opportunity for other people to talk, even if it's just to fill space. When I listen as they speak, I often get insights into what makes them special. And when I take the time to share my insights with them, I help them see it too.

Believe it or not, everyone wants to contribute; everyone wants to feel valuable. When we look for their value, we help them shine just a little bit brighter.

And the world gets a little bit better.

My Way is Not the Only Way, nor is Anyone Else's

This one was a hard one for me. I think A LOT, and because I think so much, I often think I know A LOT. This used to lead to me thinking I knew better than everyone else. I would get frustrated when people wouldn't listen or couldn't follow what I was thinking. The other challenge it would present is that I would follow MY way, even when it wasn't working. I would try to force it. I had to prove to everyone else that I was right, I was worthy, and I had value.

It was exhausting.

Accepting my unique gifts and talents, and accepting myself, meant I stopped having to prove myself all the time and opened my eyes to the fact that there is no one right way. There are as many different ways to do things as there are people, and each one has value and can be successful. Someone else's way of doing things doesn't make mine bad, just different.

When I no longer needed to justify my existence, I opened up to trying new ways, some better, some not. But with each new experience, I learn more.

Accepting that my way wasn't the only way allowed me to ask for help and receive it. It has created more ease and flow in my life. I didn't need to be in charge all the time. And it gave me more time to rest and recover, which is something a lot of us introverts need.

Conclusion

The world needs all kinds of people, and there is no one right way of being. As a leader and an introvert, it can sometimes feel like it would be easier if we were just a little louder, made a few more demands, or commanded more attention. But that simply isn't true.

One of the beautiful aspects of introverted leaders is that we can comfortably be our best selves while creating space for others to do the same. We can bring calm to chaotic situations. We give people time and space to breathe.

I also think we are a bit of a secret weapon. People often underestimate introverts for all the above-mentioned reasons. We don't call a lot of attention to ourselves, we contemplate and think to ourselves, and we don't share all of our inner thoughts. This, at times, takes the pressure off and gives us the space we need to create from our inner place of brilliance. When people already don't expect much, we don't have the added pressure of living up to expectations. This gives us the freedom to be creative and come up with unique solutions.

If you are reading this and are an introvert, I hope it has helped you see just how special and powerful you really are. I hope it has encouraged you to shine in your unique way. And I hope it has helped you see that you are perfect, just as you are!

Xo Angela

JOIN THE MOVEMENT!
#BAUW

Becoming An Unstoppable Woman
With She Rises Studios

She Rises Studios was founded by Hanna Olivas and Adriana Luna Carlos, the mother-daughter duo, in mid-2020 as they saw a need to help empower women around the world. They are the podcast hosts of the *She Rises Studios Podcast* as well as Amazon best-selling authors and motivational speakers who travel the world. Hanna and Adriana are the movement creators of #BAUW - Becoming An Unstoppable Woman: The movement has been created to universally impact women of all ages, at whatever stage of life, to overcome insecurities, and adversities, and develop an unstoppable mindset. She Rises Studios educates, celebrates, and empowers women globally.

We Are
SHE RISES STUDIOS
A real-life community of women working to become the best version of themselves to change their lives and make the world a better place.

LEARN MORE

Looking to Join Us in our Next Anthology or Publish YOUR Own?

She Rises Studios Publishing offers full-service publishing, marketing, book tour, and campaign services. For more information, contact info@sherisesstudios.com

We are always looking for women who want to share their stories and expertise and feature their businesses on our podcasts, in our books, and in our magazines.

SEE WHAT WE DO

OUR PODCAST

OUR BOOKS

OUR SERVICES

Be featured in the Becoming An Unstoppable Woman magazine, published in 13 countries and sold in all major retailers. Get the visibility you need to LEVEL UP in your business!

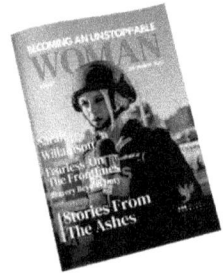

Have your own TV show streamed across major platforms like Roku TV, Amazon Fire Stick, Apple TV and more!

Learn to leverage your expertise. Build your online presence and grow your audience with Fenix TV.
https://fenixtv.sherisesstudios.com/

Visit www.SheRisesStudios.com to see how YOU can join the #BAUW movement and help your community to achieve the UNSTOPPABLE mindset.

Have you checked out the *She Rises Studios Podcast?*

Find us on all MAJOR platforms: Spotify, IHeartRadio, Apple Podcasts, Google Podcasts, etc.

Looking to become a sponsor or build a partnership?

Email us at info@sherisesstudios.com

SHE RISES
STUDIOS

www.ingramcontent.com/pod-product-compliance
Lightning Source LLC
Chambersburg PA
CBHW060258030426

42335CB00014B/1768